West-Malbuch

Cowboys

Coloring Pages for Kids

Coloring Pages for Kids
An imprint of Ciparum LLC

West-Malbuch Cowboys
© 2017 Ciparum LLC
All rights reserved.
ISBN-10:1-63589-430-1
ISBN-13:978-1-63589-430-1

Coloring Pages for Kids

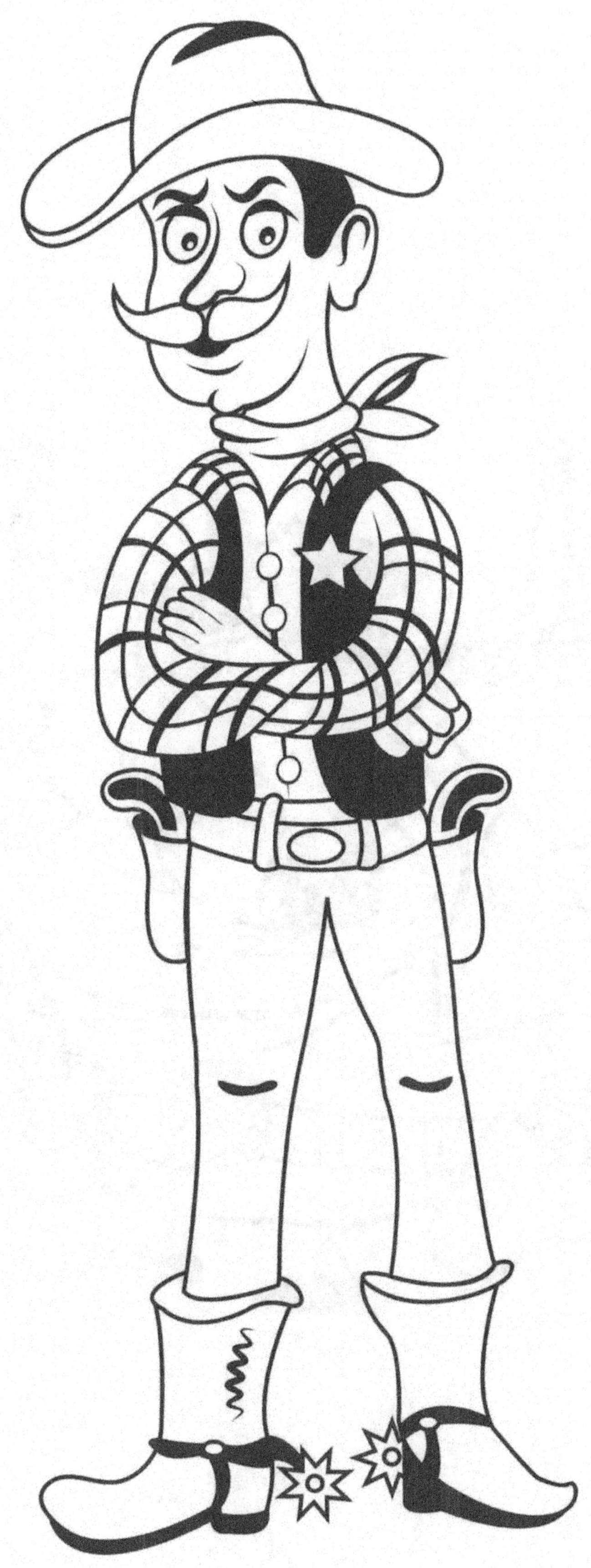

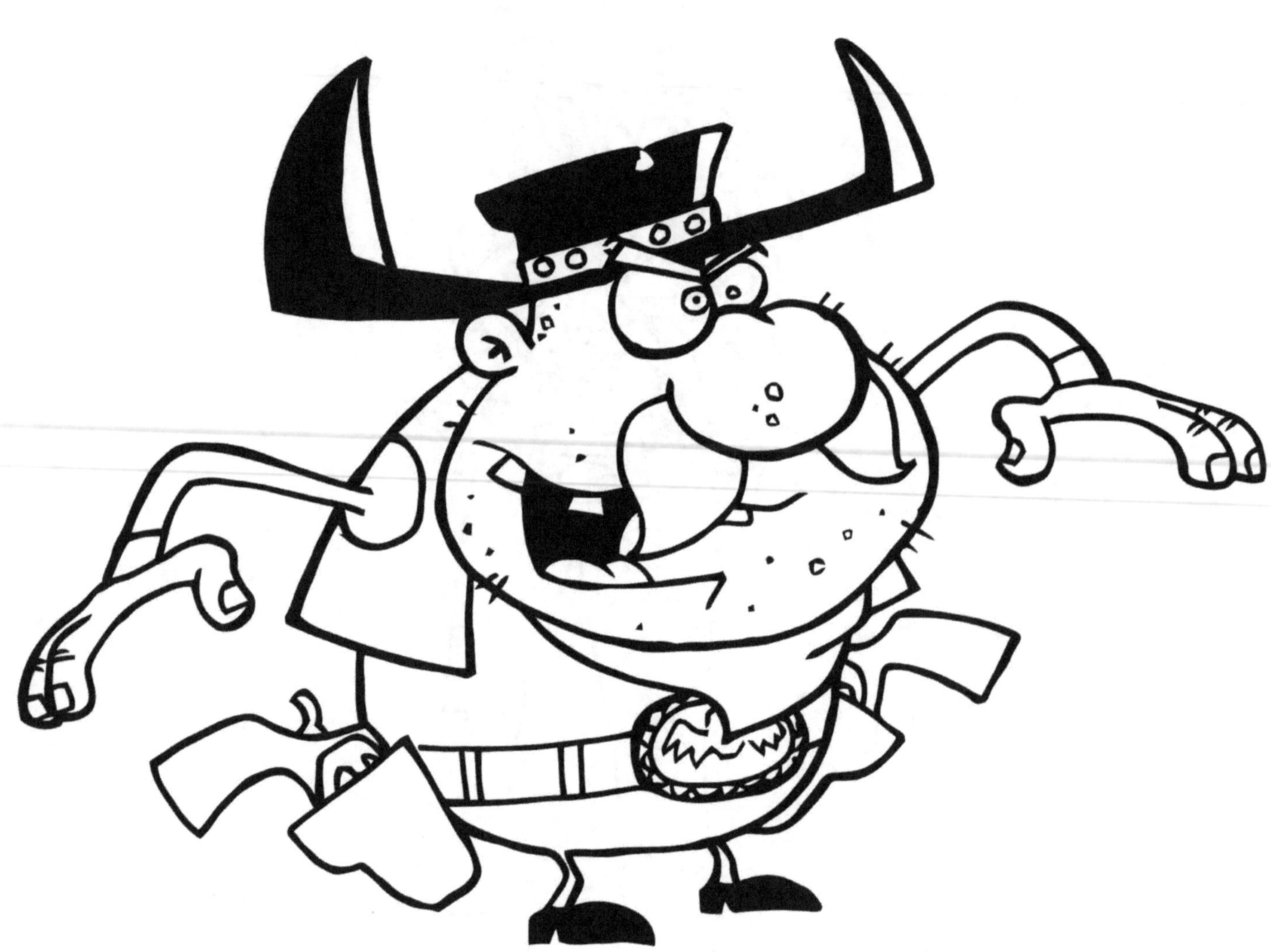

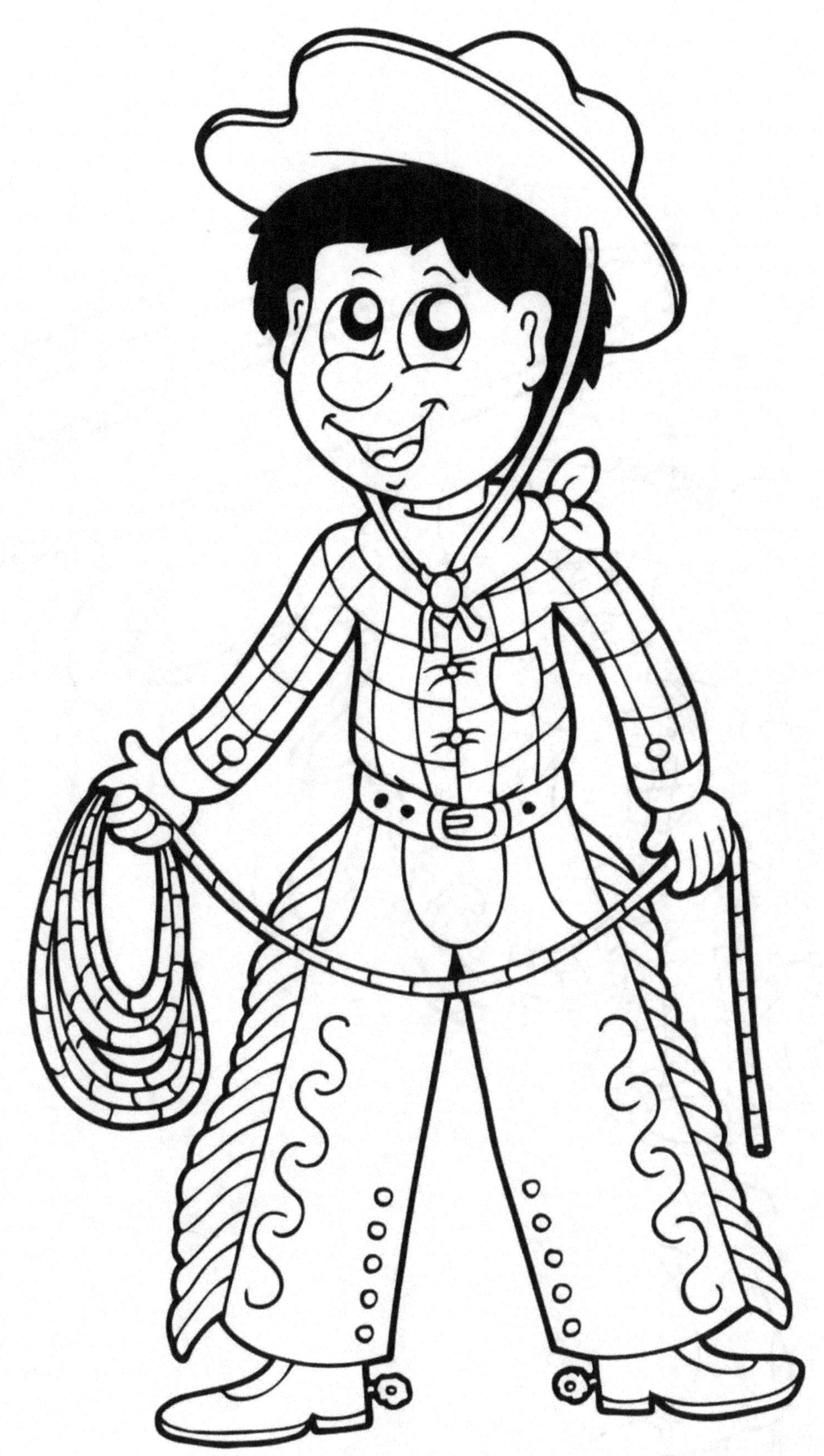

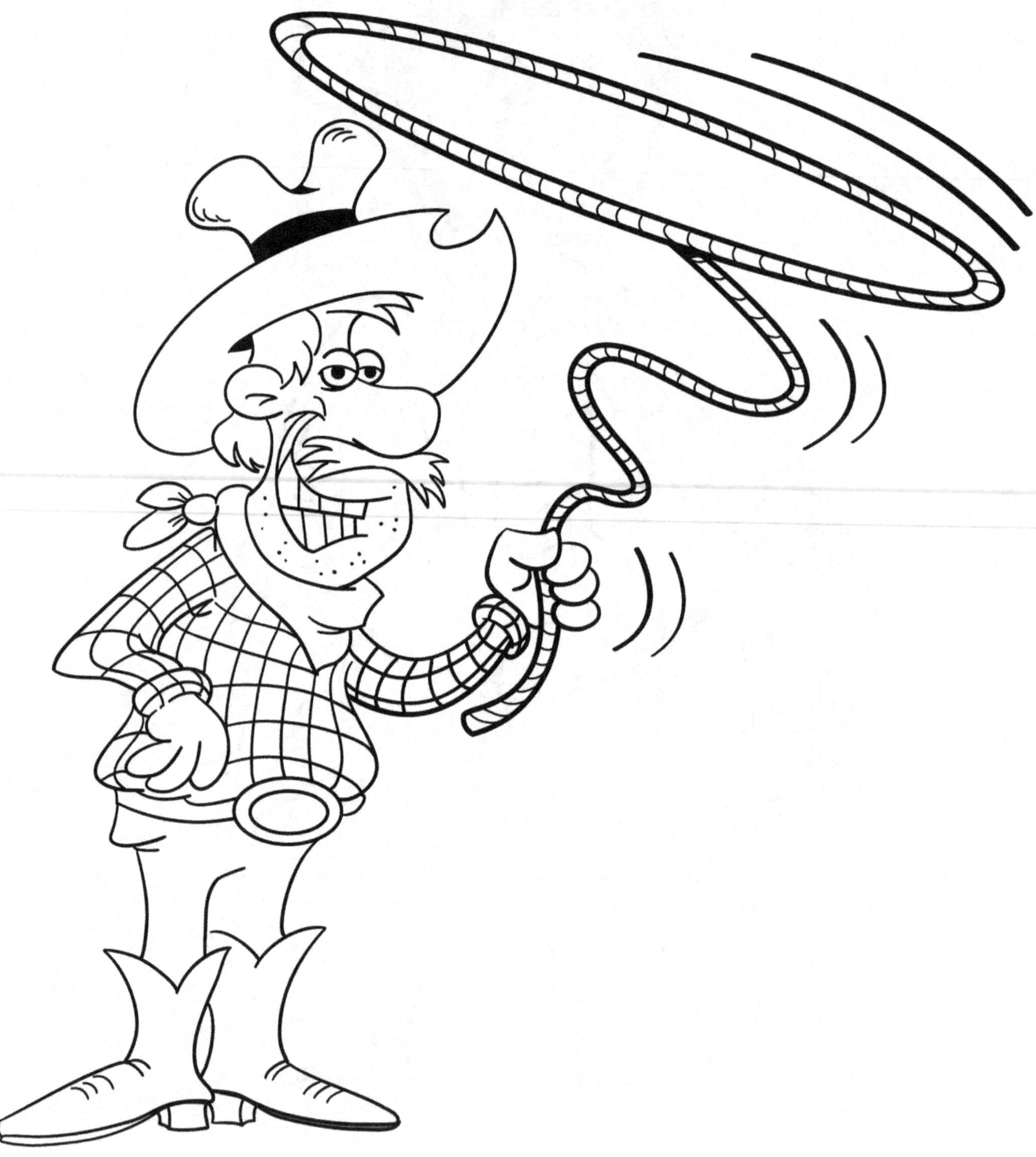

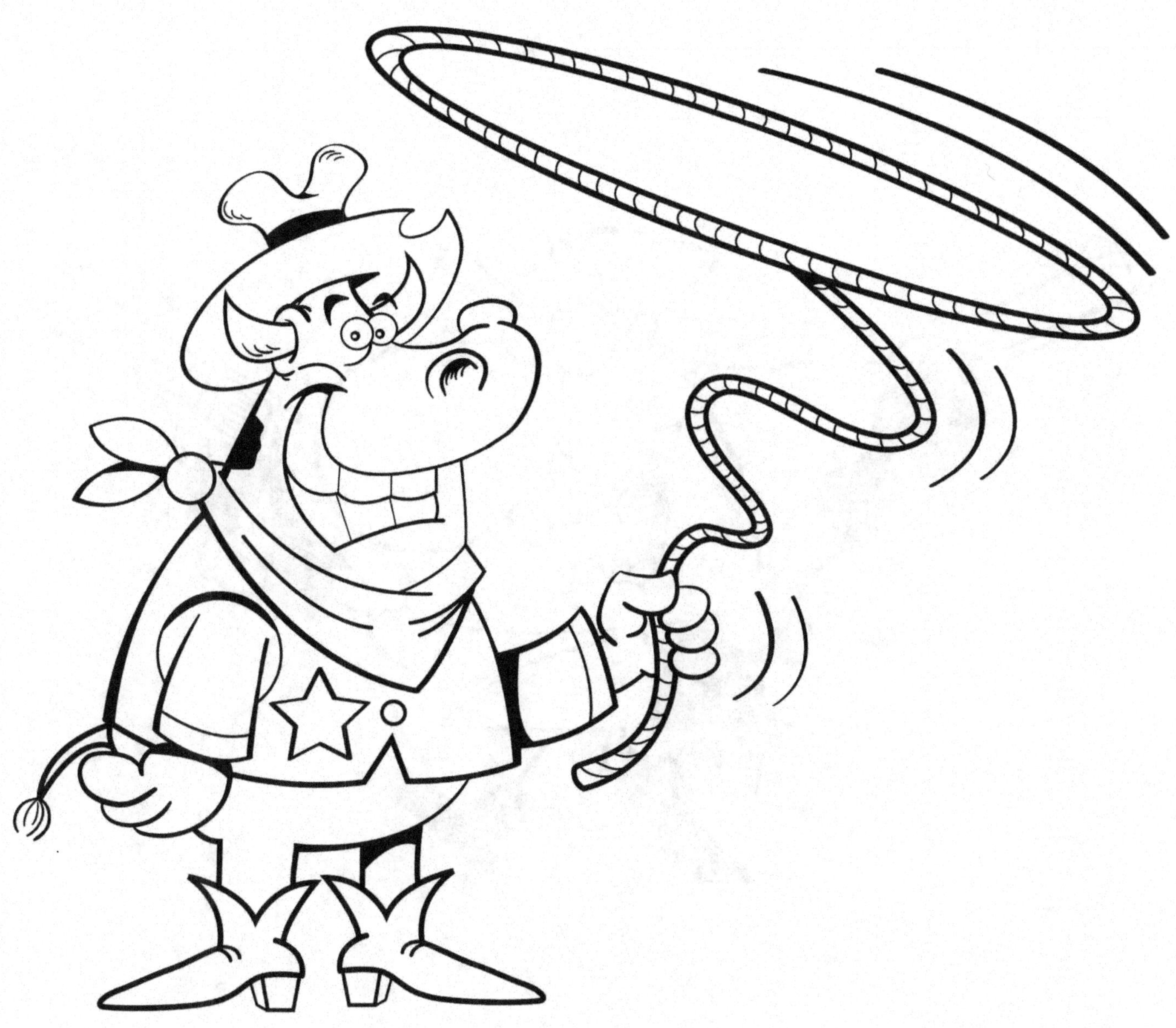

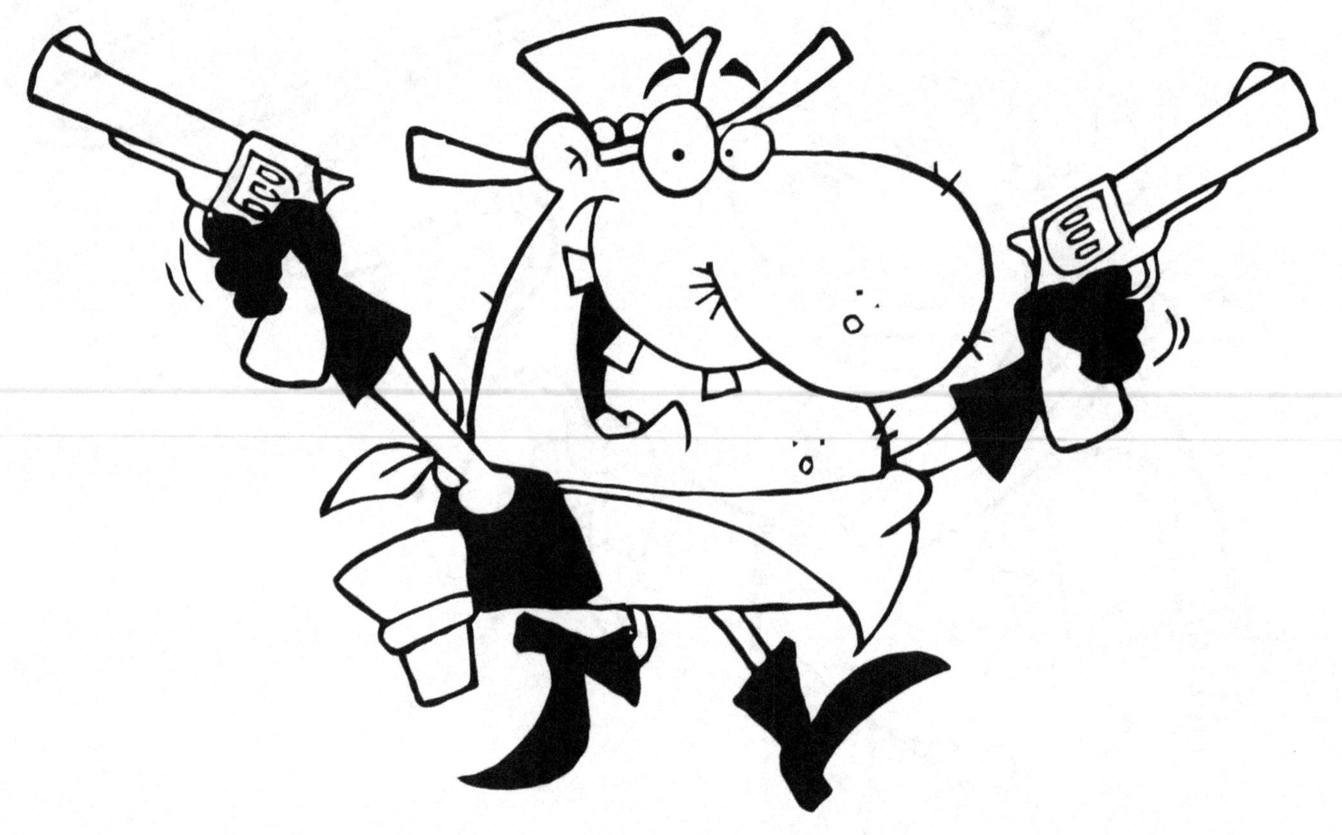

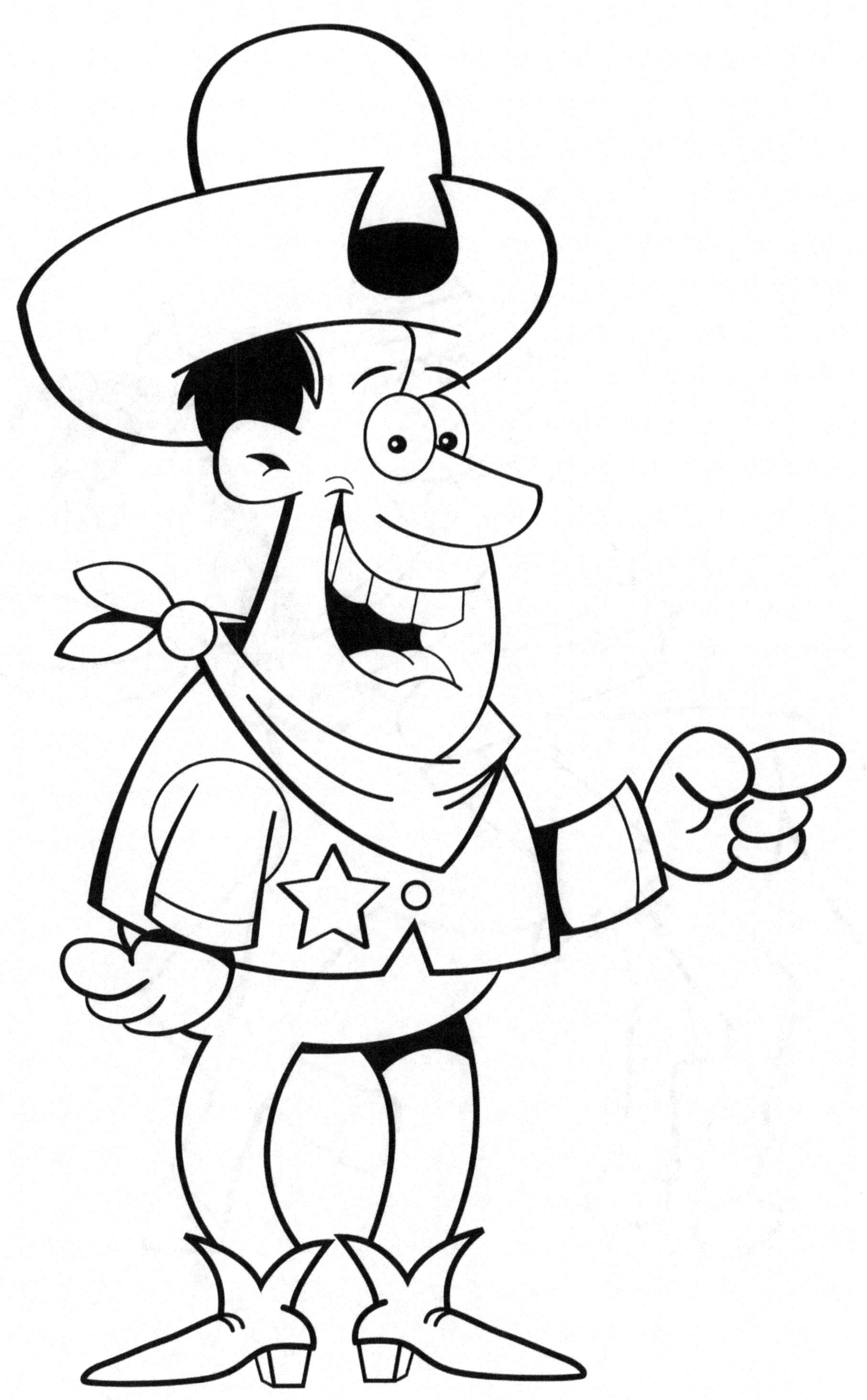

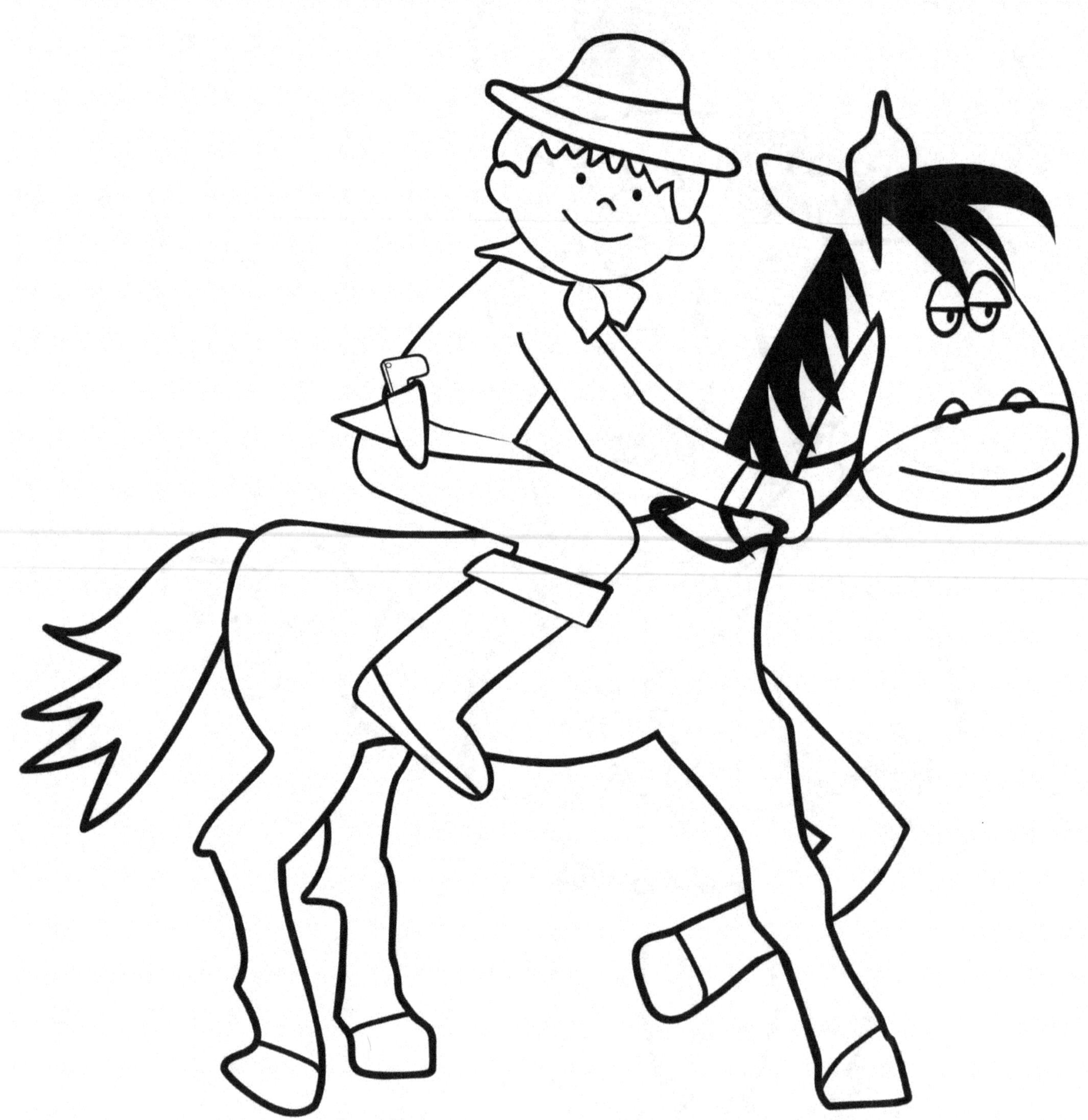

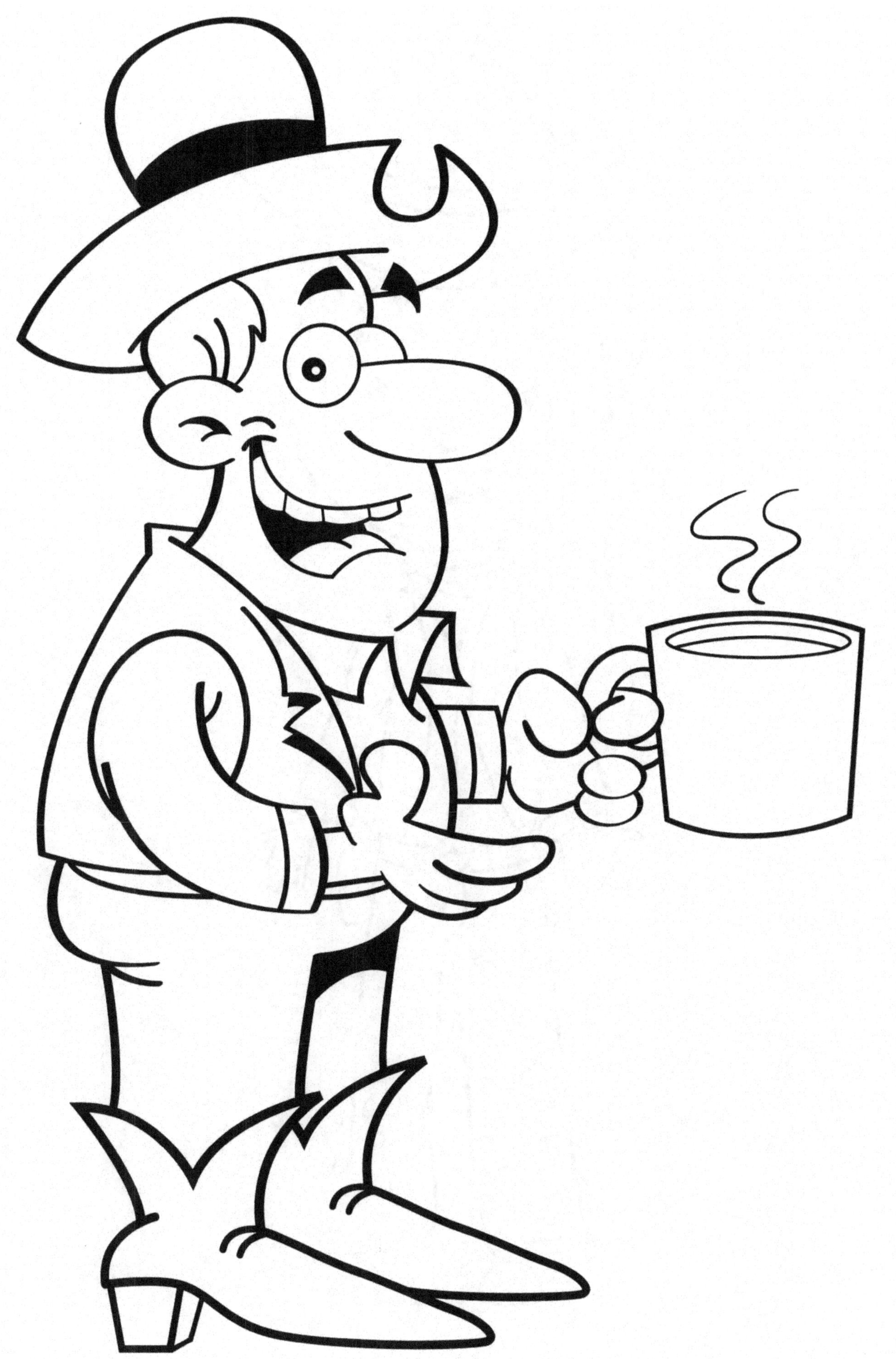

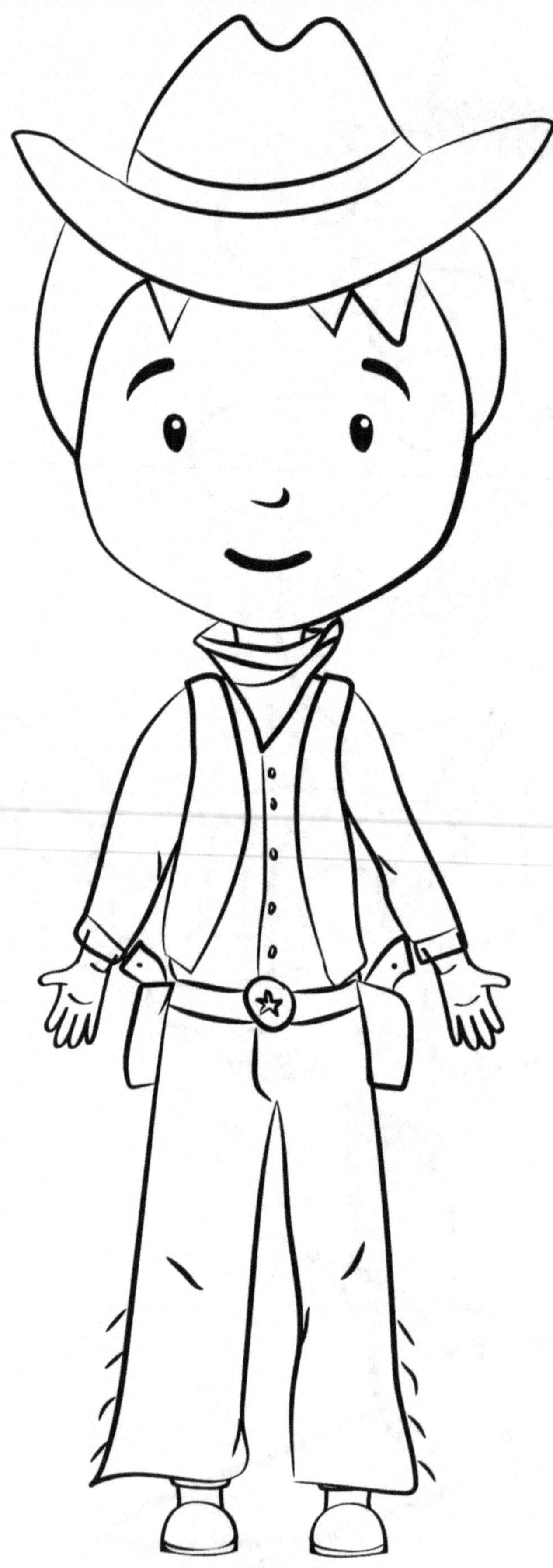

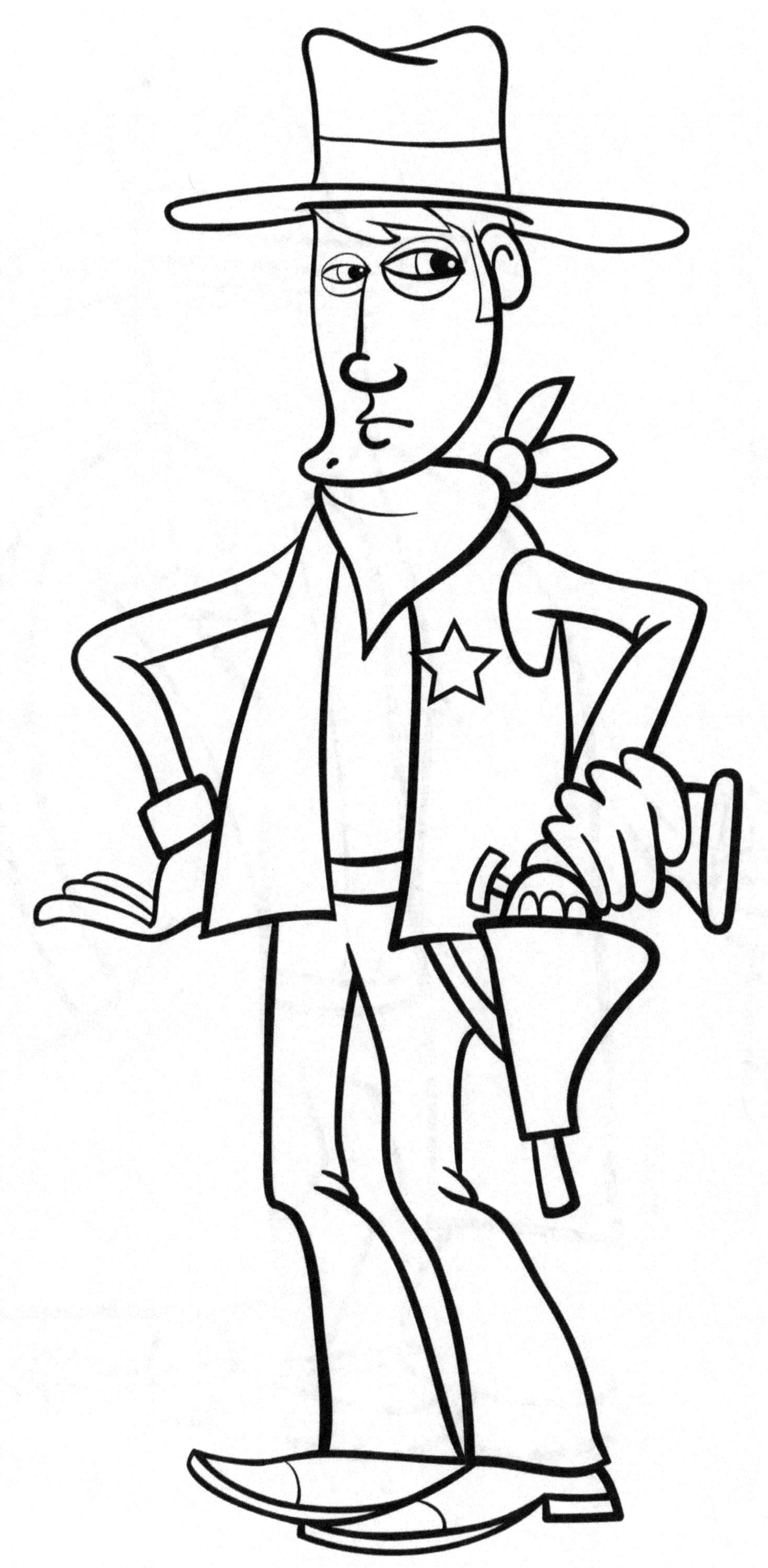

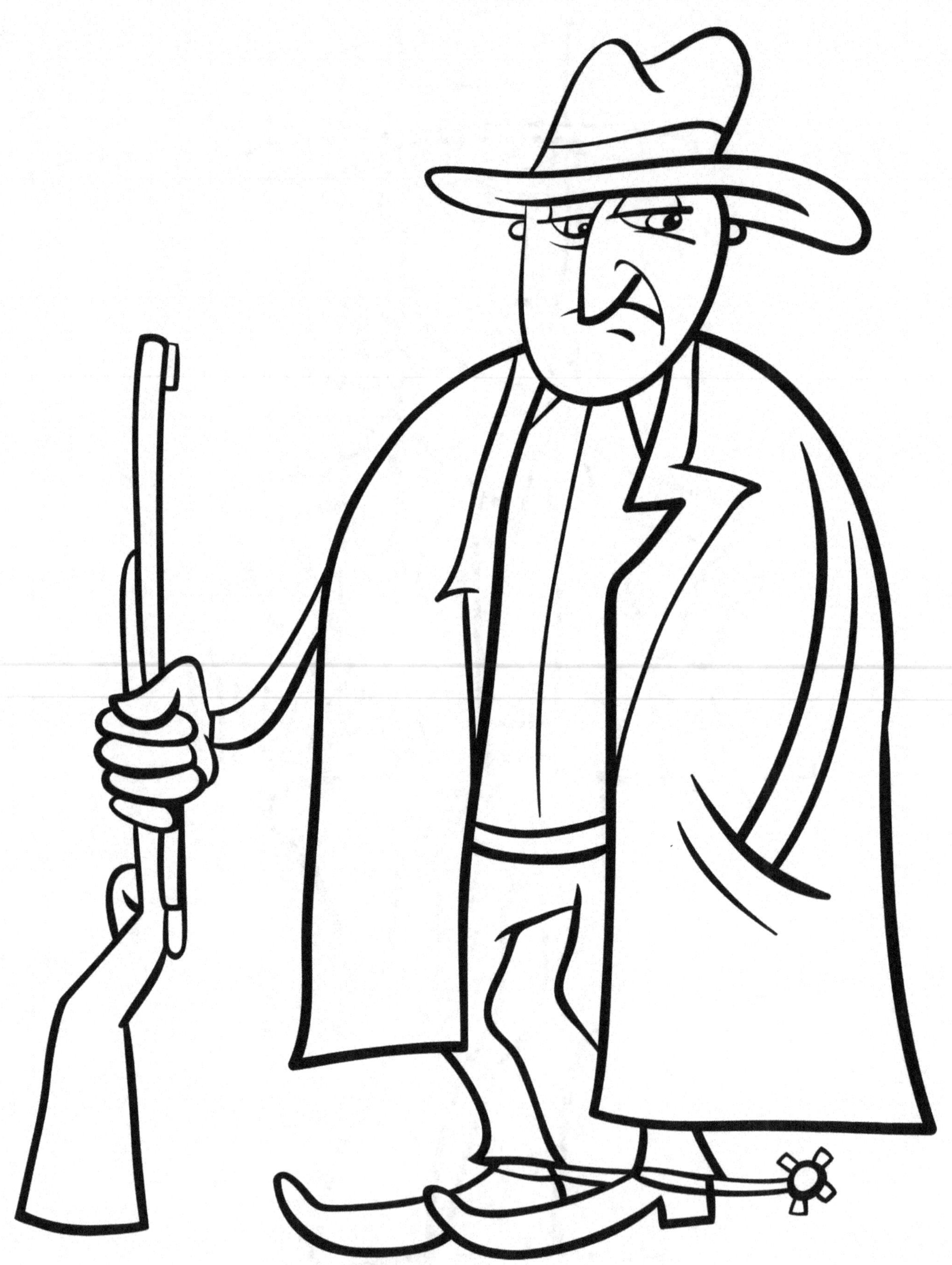

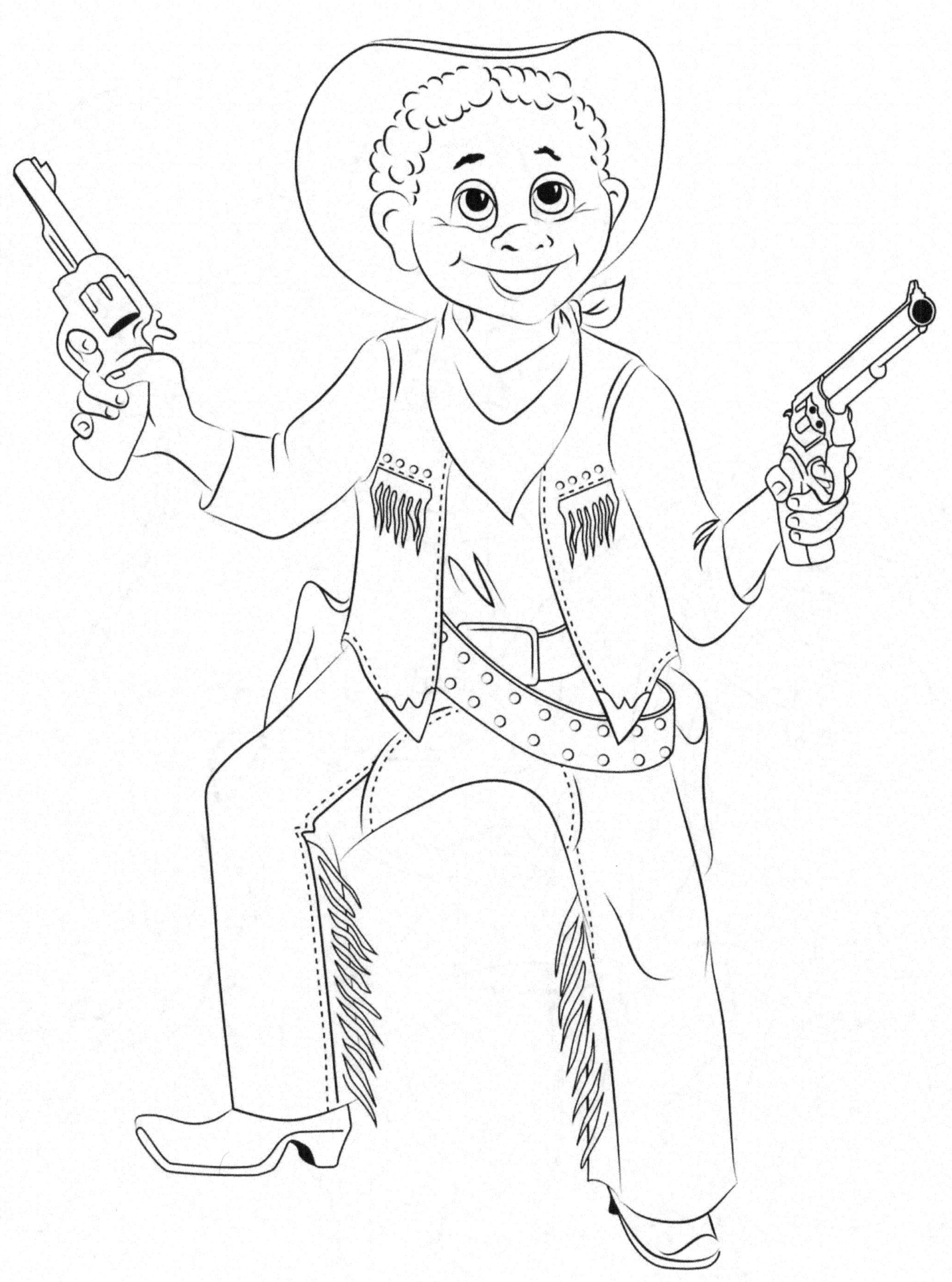

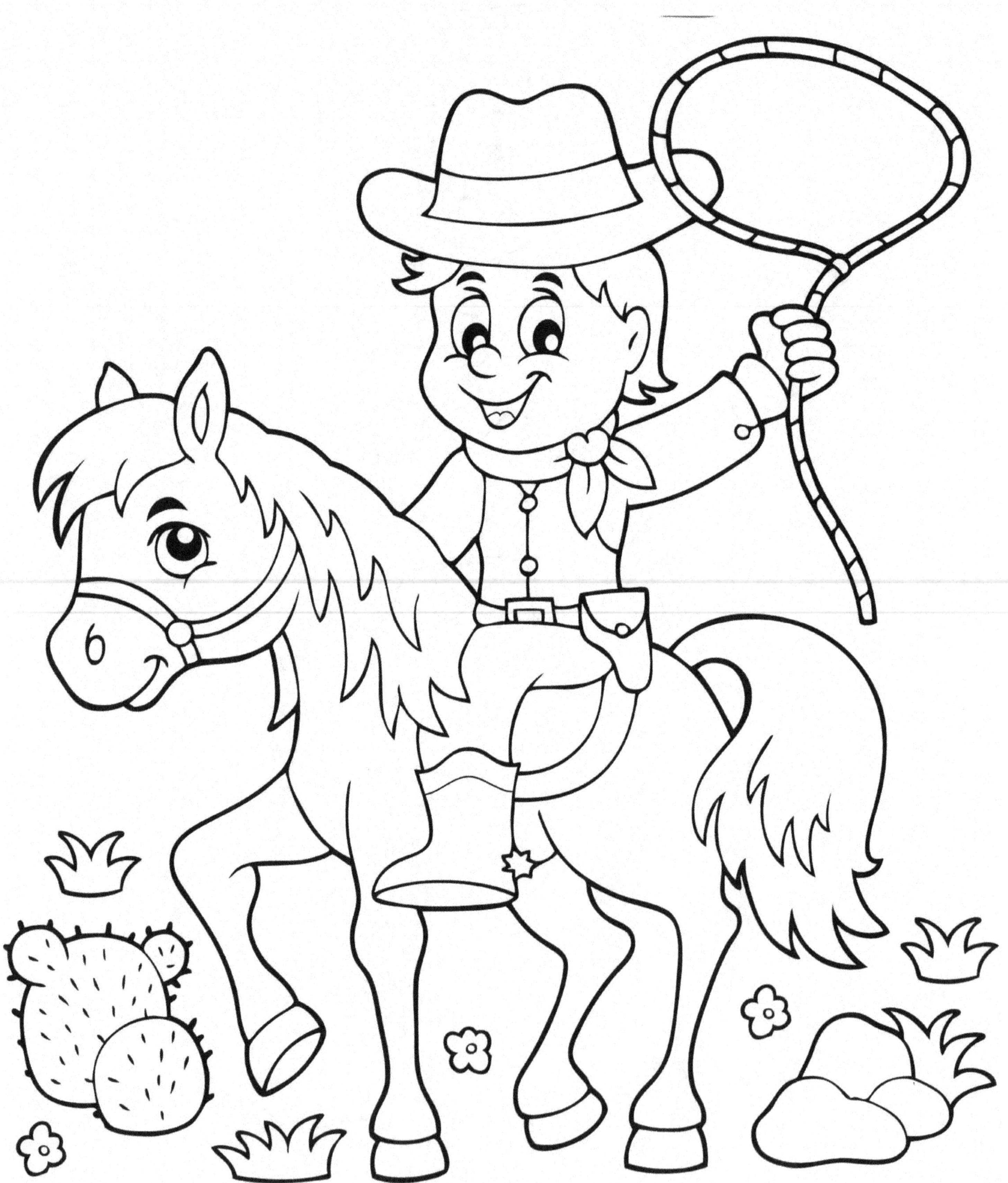

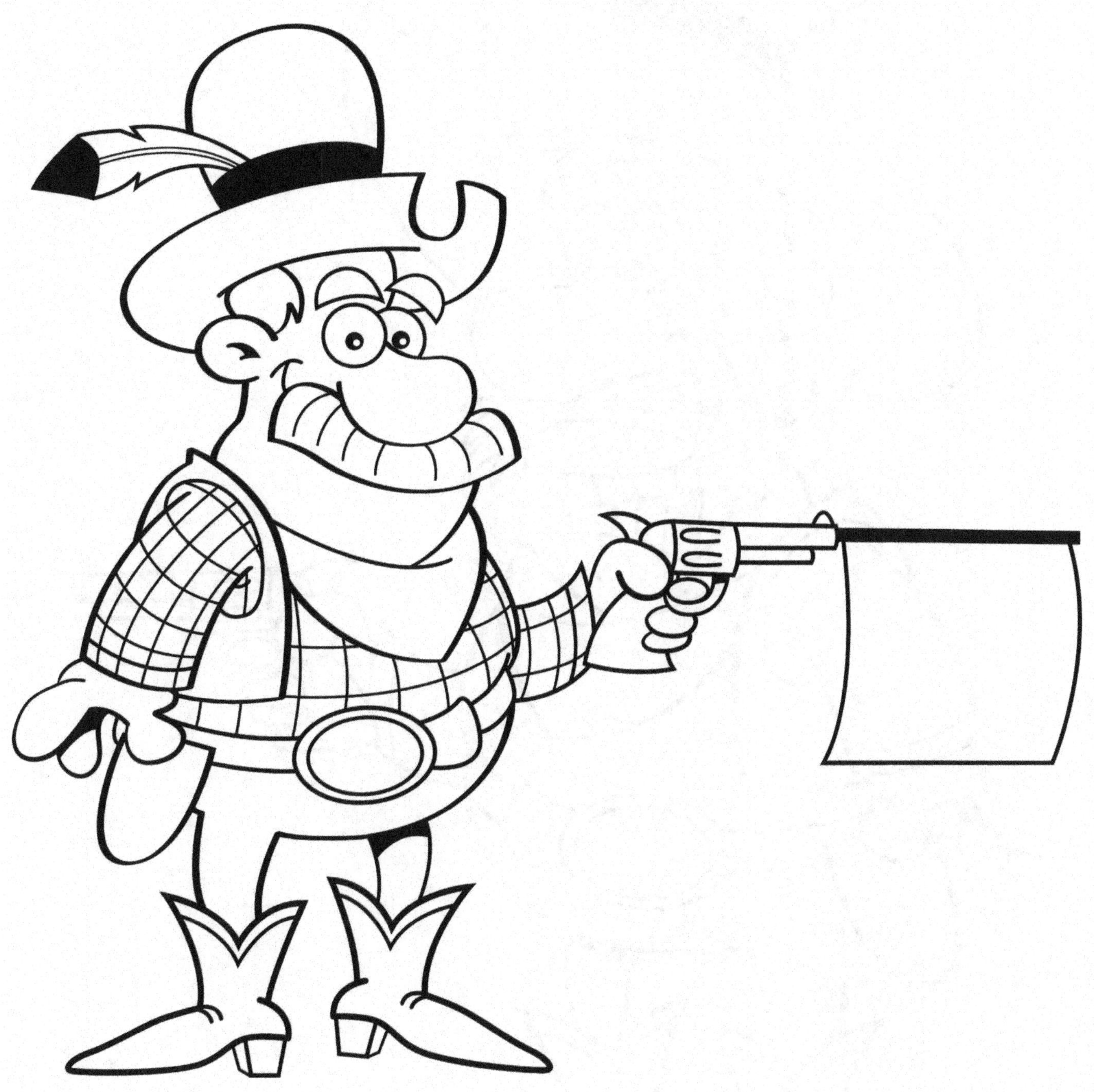

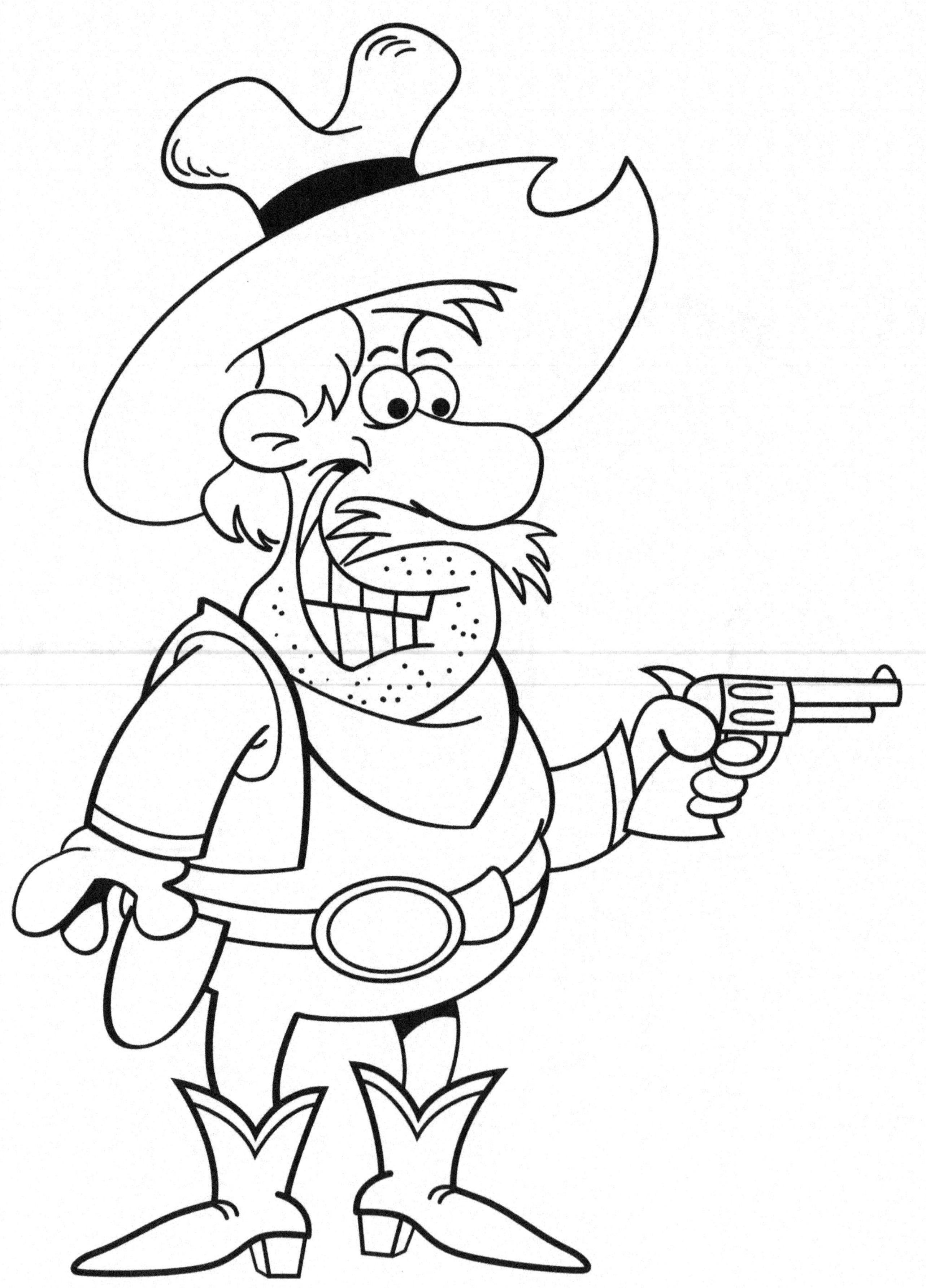

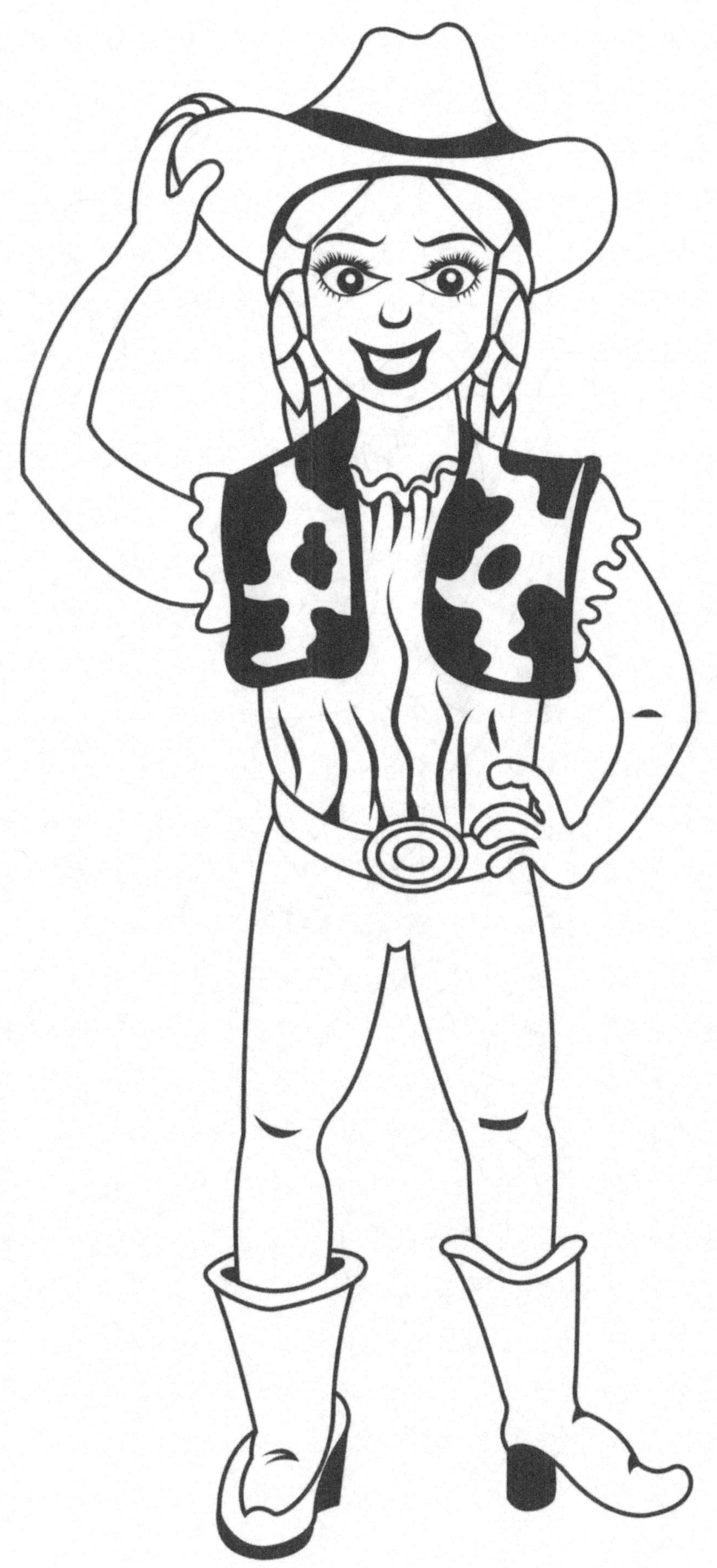

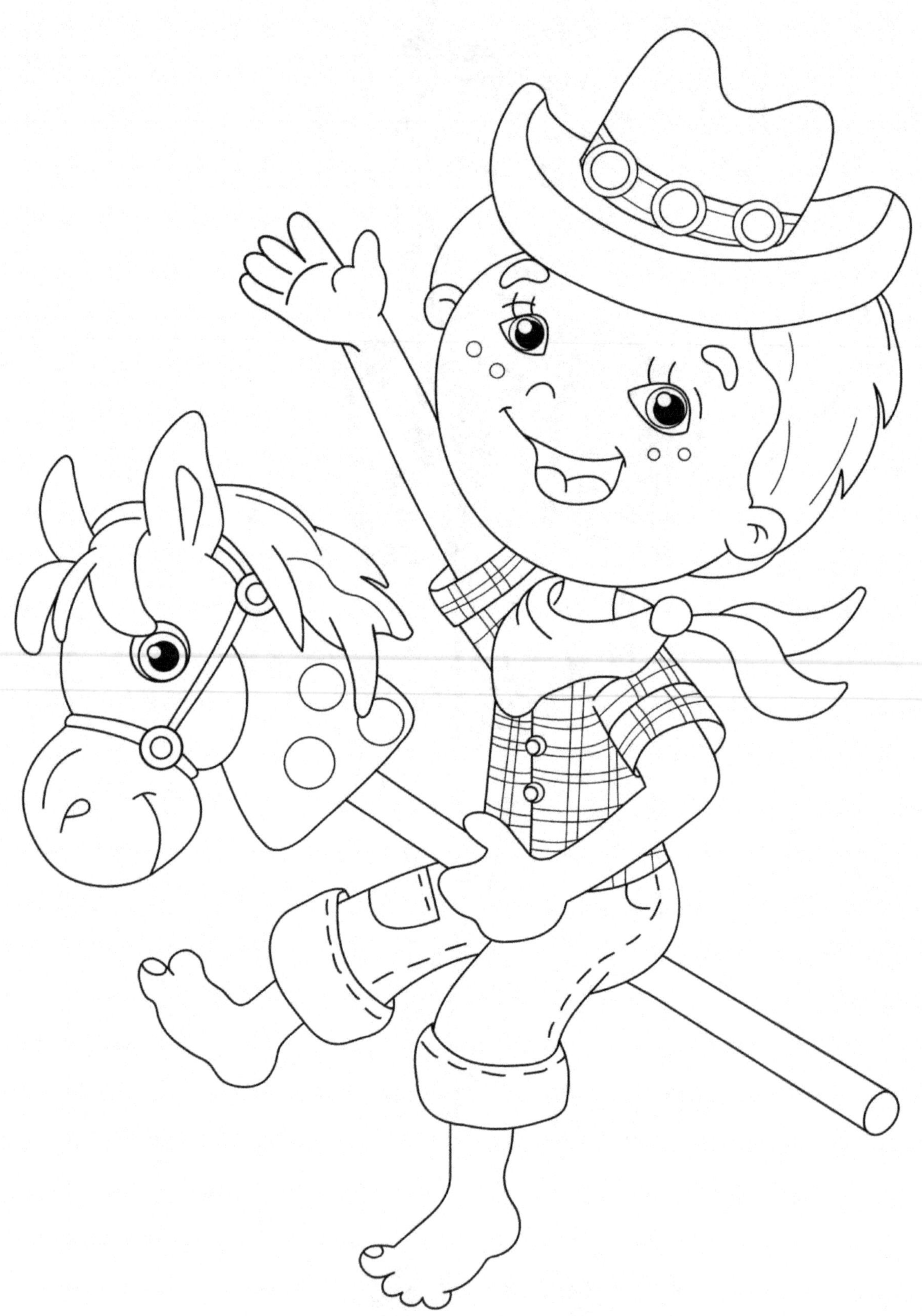

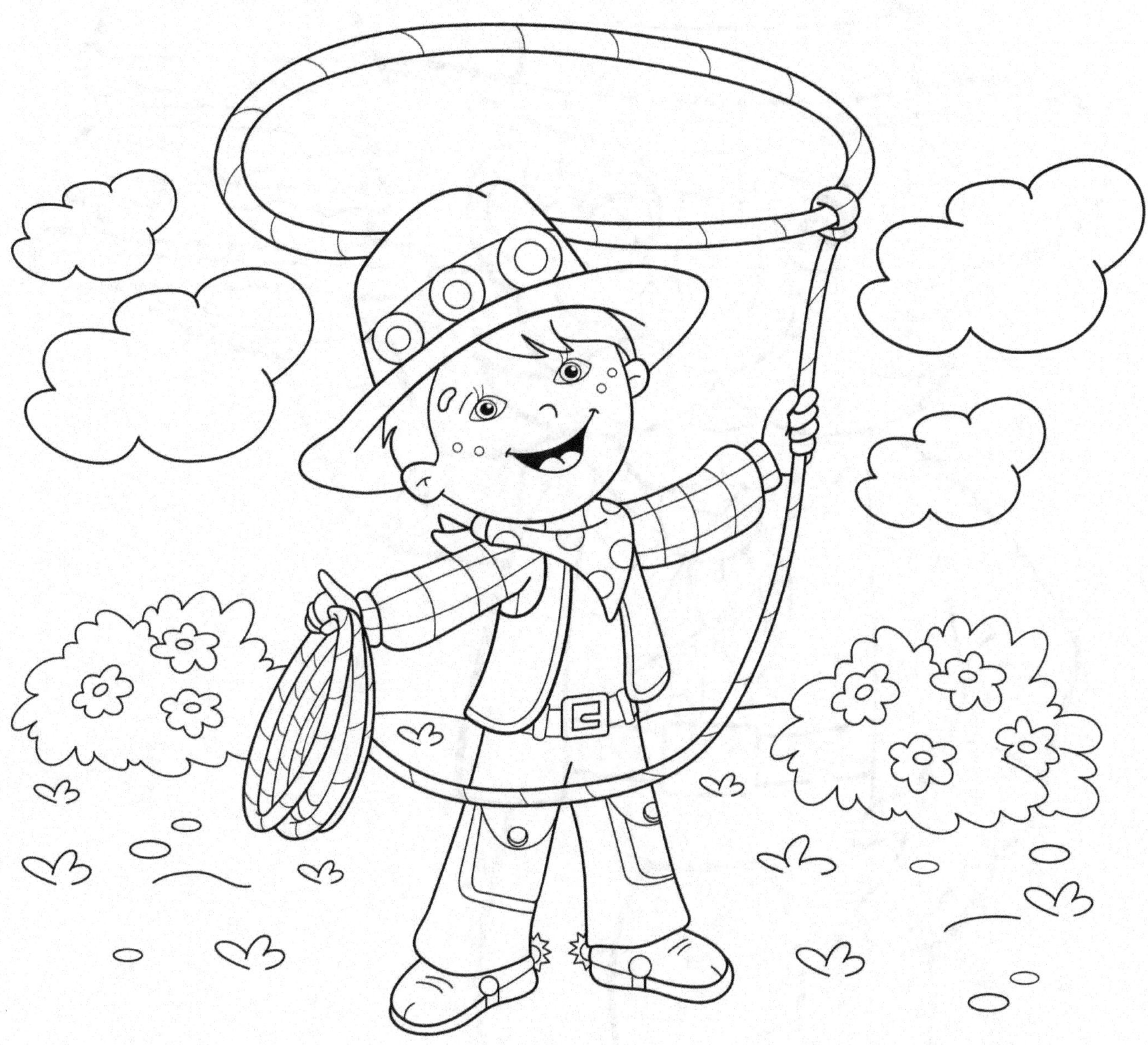

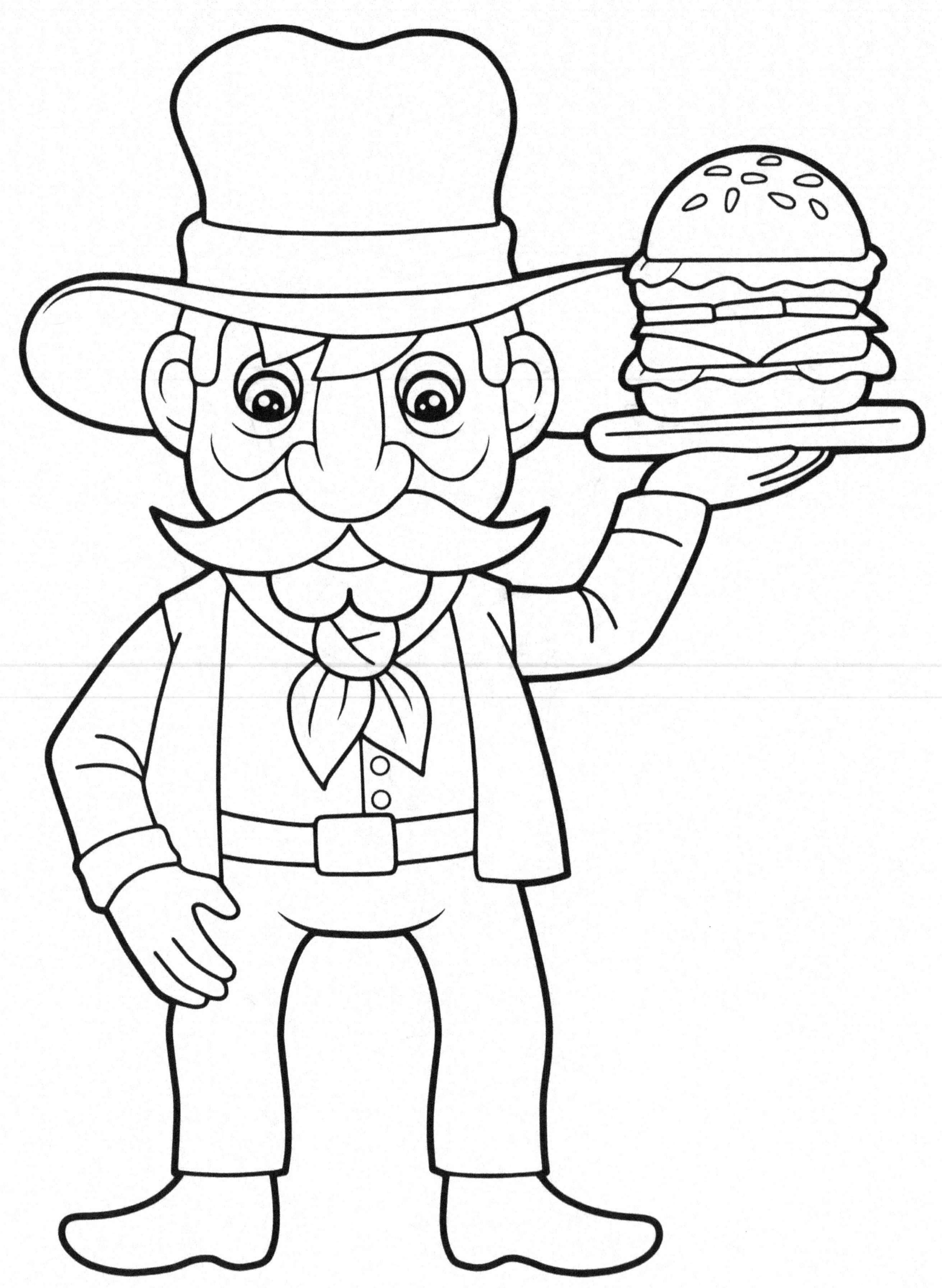

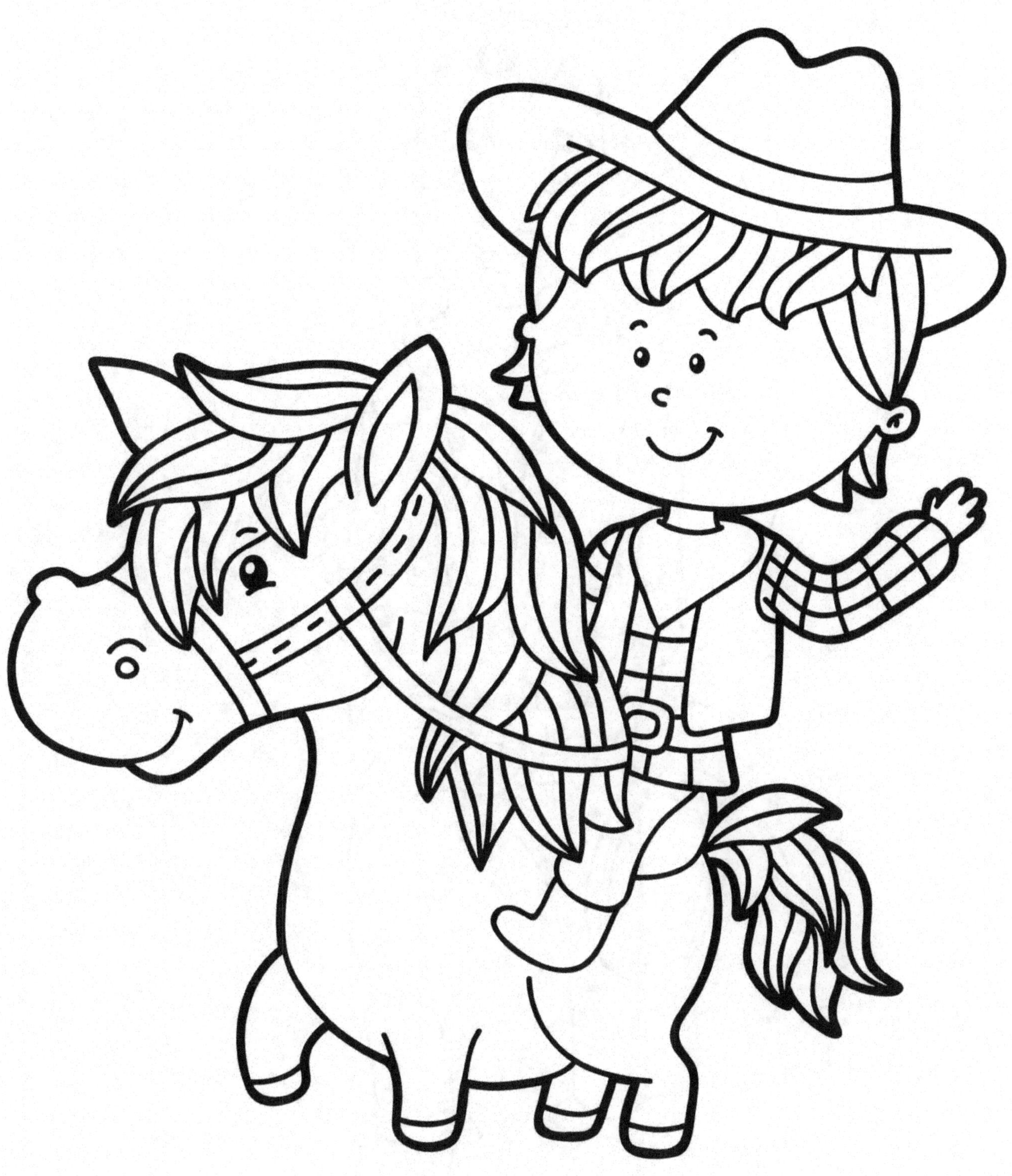

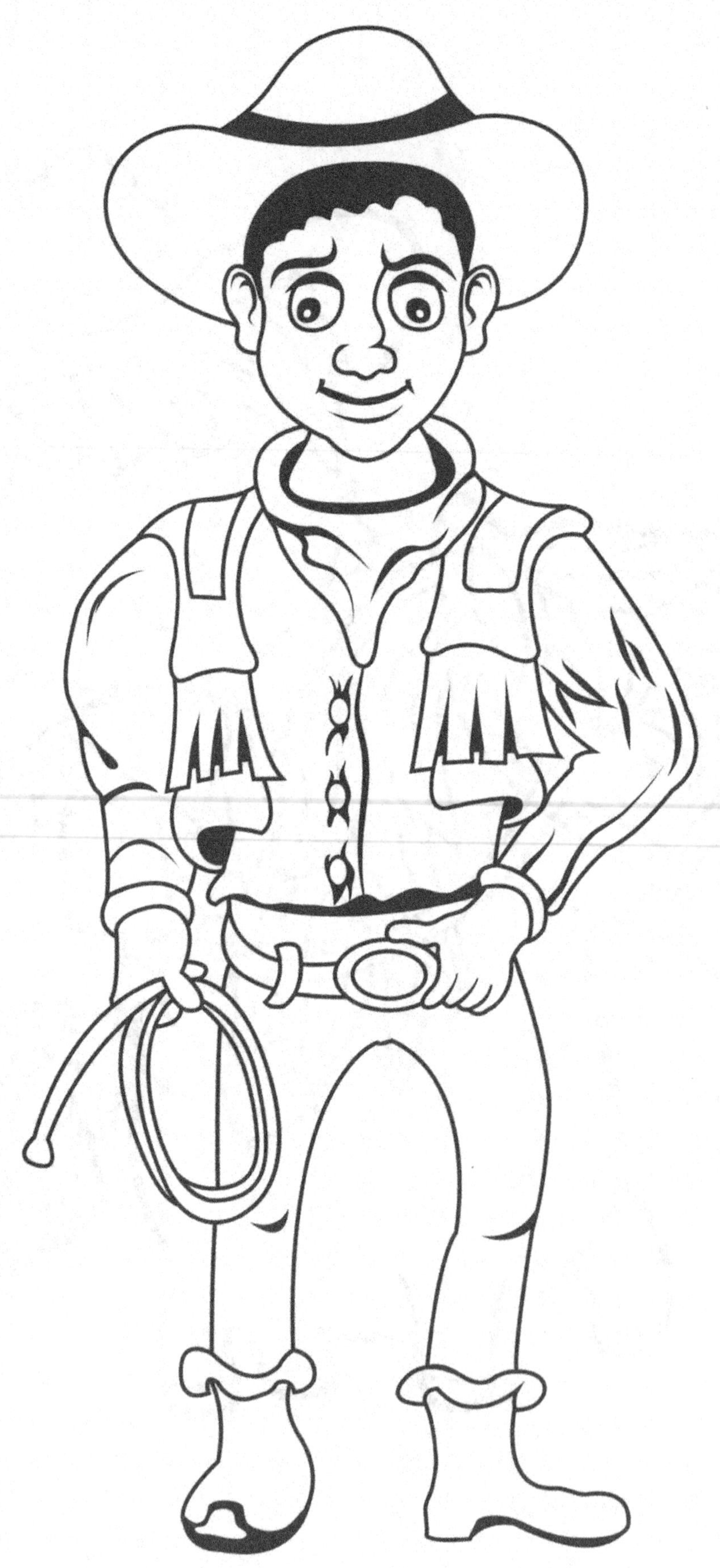